# Table of Content

I0446318

# Table of Contents

# Introduction

The concept of credit can be traced back to the agrarian societies of ancient civilizations; however, the structured system of credit as we know it began to take shape in the United States in the late 19th century. Initially, credit was a localized system, primarily based on personal relationships and trust between merchants and their customers. Store owners extended credit to known individuals within the community, relying on verbal agreements and character assessments.

The increasing mobility of the American population in the 1800s and the expansion of commerce highlighted the need for a more standardized and reliable credit system. In response, the first credit reporting agency, the Mercantile Agency, was founded in 1841 by Lewis Tappan. This agency collected information on individuals and businesses to assess their creditworthiness, setting the foundation for the modern credit reporting system.

As the American economy grew and evolved, so did the credit system. The early 20th century witnessed the establishment of credit bureaus, the precursors to the major

1

credit bureaus we are familiar with today: Equifax, Experian, and TransUnion. These bureaus collected, updated, and sold credit information to subscribers, mainly merchants and lenders.

The invention of the credit score in the 1950s by engineer William R. Fair and mathematician Earl J. Isaac marked a significant milestone. Their scoring system, FICO (Fair Isaac Corporation), used mathematical algorithms to calculate a person's credit risk, revolutionizing credit lending by providing a standardized and objective measure of creditworthiness.

The introduction of the Diners Club card in 1950 marked the beginning of the credit card era. Initially intended for travel and entertainment expenses, credit cards gained immense popularity, creating Visa and Mastercard. The availability of credit cards enabled consumers to make purchases and pay for them over time, contributing to the rise of consumer spending and debt.

The Equal Credit Opportunity Act of 1974 and the advent of securitization in the 1980s further expanded access to credit. These developments democratized credit, making it available to a wider demographic, while also fueling economic growth through increased consumer spending and the development of mortgage-backed and asset-backed securities.

The rise of the internet and advancements in technology in the late 20th and early 21st centuries ushered in a new era for credit in the United States. Online banking and lending became prevalent, providing consumers with greater access to financial services and credit. Financial technology companies, or FinTechs, leveraged big data and analytics to assess credit risk, offering alternative lending solutions and further democratizing credit access.

The 2008 financial crisis highlighted the vulnerabilities and risks inherent in the credit system. The crisis, fueled by subprime mortgage lending and excessive risk-taking, led to a re-evaluation of lending practices and regulations. The Dodd–Frank Wall Street Reform and Consumer Protection Act of 2010 introduced comprehensive financial reforms, including establishing the Consumer Financial Protection Bureau (CFPB), aimed at protecting consumers and maintaining the financial system's integrity.

As we move further into the 21st century, the credit landscape continues to evolve. Developments in artificial intelligence, blockchain technology, and decentralized finance (DeFi) are poised to shape the future of credit in the United States. The increasing emphasis on financial inclusion and responsible lending practices, coupled with technological innovation, suggests a dynamic and inclusive future for credit.

The journey of credit in the United States has been multifaceted and transformative. Credit has played a pivotal role in shaping the economic landscape from its rudimentary beginnings as a trust-based system to the sophisticated, technology-driven structure we see today. Understanding the history and evolution of credit provides valuable insights into its integral role in individual financial empowerment and economic development. This introduction has aimed to provide a comprehensive overview of the inception, evolution, and future trajectory of credit in the United States, setting the stage for a deeper exploration of its various components and their impact on consumers and the economy.

# Chapter 1: Understanding Credit Scores

*"Understanding your credit score is akin to understanding the key to unlocking financial opportunities. It's the first step towards financial literacy and, ultimately, financial freedom."*

## 1.1 What are Credit Scores?

A credit score is a three-digit numerical expression representing a person's creditworthiness. It's calculated based on your credit files and financial history, which include your borrowing history, payment behavior, and current outstanding debts. Lenders, landlords, and even some employers use credit scores to predict their risk when lending money, renting out property, or hiring a new employee.

## 1.2 How do Credit Scores Work?

Credit scores are not static; they constantly change as new financial information is added to your credit report. For example, when you pay off a loan, miss a payment, or take on new debt, your credit score will change to reflect these activities. The algorithms that calculate credit scores are complex and proprietary, meaning they've closely guarded the secrets of the companies that create them. However, we do know that they consider various factors from your credit report, including your payment history, the amount of debt you owe, the length of your credit history, new credit, and the types of credit used.

## 1.3 The Range of Credit Scores

The US's most used credit score model is the FICO score, named after the Fair Isaac Corporation, which developed it. FICO scores range from 300 to 850, with 850 being the best possible score.

- Poor Credit: 300-579
- Fair Credit: 580-669
- Good Credit: 670-739
- Very Good Credit: 740-799
- Exceptional Credit: 800-850

Remember that these ranges can vary slightly depending on the credit bureau and scoring model.

## 1.4 What Makes a Good Credit Score?

The higher your credit score, the less risk you pose to lenders and the more likely you will be approved for loans and credit cards at the most favorable terms. Generally, a score above 670 (on the FICO scale) is considered good. However, to get the best interest rates and loan terms, you might aim for a score of 740 or above.

## 1.5 Factors that Influence Your Credit Score

Several factors influence your credit score. Here are the main ones, according to FICO:

**Payment History (35%):** This is the most significant factor. It considers if you've paid your bills on time, had any late payments, and how late they were.

**Amounts Owed (30%):** This is also known as credit utilization. It's the ratio of your outstanding debt to your total available credit.

**Length of Credit History (15%):** The longer your credit history, the better your score can be. This factor looks at the age of your oldest account, your newest account, and the average age of all your accounts.

**Credit Mix (10%):** This considers the different types of credit you have, such as credit cards, retail accounts, installment loans, mortgage loans, etc.

**New Credit (10%):** This includes the number of recently opened accounts and recent inquiries from lenders. Too many new accounts or hard inquiries can negatively affect your score.

Understanding the intricacies of credit scoring is the first crucial step towards aiming for a perfect 850. It provides the foundation to comprehend where you currently stand, the factors affecting your credit score, and the steps needed to enhance your credit profile. While achieving an 850-credit score might seem daunting, it's not impossible. However, it's worth noting that it's a feat only a small percentage of Americans have achieved. According to FICO data, as of 2021, only about 1.2% of Americans have a perfect 850 credit score. Remember, while perfection is admirable, what's most important is having a score that can get you the best possible deals, and for most people, that can happen well below 850. On this journey, each step toward improving your credit moves you towards better financial health and freedom.

# Chapter 2: The Anatomy of Your Credit Report

*"Mastering the anatomy of your credit report is like learning the language of your financial health; once fluent, you'll gain the power to shape your financial future."*

## 2.1 What is a Credit Report?

A credit report is a detailed record of your credit history compiled by credit bureaus. The information in your credit report is used to calculate your credit score. It includes details about your credit accounts, payment history, and public records.

## 2.2 The Different Sections of a Credit Report

Your credit report is divided into several sections, each containing different types of information:

**1. Personal Information:** This section includes your name, current and previous addresses, Social Security number, date of birth, and potentially your employment information. This information is used to identify you, not to calculate your credit score.

**2. Credit Accounts (or Trade Lines):** This section lists all your credit accounts, including credit cards, auto loans, mortgages, and other types of credit you've obtained. For each account, the report will include the type of account, the date it was opened, your credit limit or loan amount, the account balance, and your payment history.

**3. Credit Inquiries:** This section lists everyone who accessed your credit report within the past two years. There are two types of inquiries: hard and soft. Hard inquiries occur when you apply for new credit and can slightly lower your credit score for a short period. Soft inquiries include requests to see your credit report and do not affect your score.

**4. Public Records and Collections:** This section includes information about bankruptcies, foreclosures, lawsuits, wage garnishments, liens, and judgments. It may also include information about overdue debt from collection agencies.

## 2.3 Obtaining a Copy of Your Credit Report

Under federal law, you're entitled to a free copy of your credit report from each of the three credit reporting bureaus—Equifax, Experian, and TransUnion—once every 12 months. You can obtain these reports through AnnualCreditReport.com, the only website federally authorized to provide these free reports. Outside of this, a report can be requested directly from the credit bureaus, usually for a fee, unless you meet specific criteria like being denied credit.

## 2.4 Reviewing Your Credit Report Regularly

Regularly reviewing your credit report is essential to managing and improving your credit. It allows you to catch and correct any errors that might lower your score. Additionally, it can also help you detect signs of identity theft early.

## 2.5 Interpreting Information in Your Credit Report

When reviewing your credit report, pay close attention to the credit accounts and payment history sections, as they make up a significant portion of your credit score. Ensure that all the accounts listed are yours, the balances are correct, and your payment history matches your records.

Remember, your credit report doesn't just influence your ability to get credit. It can affect many aspects of your life, from getting a job to how much you pay for insurance. Understanding how to read and interpret your credit report is critical in managing your overall financial health.

# Chapter 3: Identifying & Rectifying Errors on Your Credit Report

*"In the pursuit of credit perfection, vigilance is your greatest ally. Be meticulous in examining your credit report, steadfast in challenging errors, and diligent in tracking corrections - for in this accuracy lies the key to your optimum credit score."*

## 3.1 Identifying Errors on Your Credit Report

Errors on your credit report can range from simple clerical errors to severe mistakes, such as accounts that aren't yours, which could indicate identity theft. Some common types of errors include:

- **Identity Errors:** These can be as simple as wrong name spelling, phone number, or address or as serious as mix-ups between individuals with similar names.

- **Incorrect Account Status:** This includes closed accounts reported as open, being listed as the account owner when you are an authorized user, wrong dates related to account opening or closing, and other similar mistakes.

- **Data Management Errors:** These occur when the same debt is listed more than once, creating the illusion of a higher level of debt.

- **Balance Errors:** These are simply inaccuracies in the amount you owe on an account.

Identifying these errors involves thoroughly checking your credit report, line by line, to verify that the information listed is correct.

## 3.2 How to Dispute Errors

If you find errors on your credit report, it's important to dispute them as soon as possible. Here are the steps to take:

1. **Write a Dispute Letter:** This letter should identify each item in your report you dispute, state the facts, explain why you dispute the information, and request that it be removed or corrected.

2. **Attach Supporting Documents:** Include copies (not originals) of documents that support your position.

3. **Send the Letter by Certified Mail:** It's crucial to have proof that you sent the dispute, so send the letter by certified mail, return receipt requested.

4. **Contact the Creditor:** In addition to the credit bureau, send the dispute letter and supporting documents to the creditor who provided the information.

**Note:** In later chapters, we are going to show how to leverage artificial intelligence to complete these steps for you.

## 3.3 Keeping Track of the Dispute Process

Once you've sent the dispute letter, the credit bureau must investigate your claim, usually within 30 days. They'll forward your dispute to the creditor, who must review your claim and report to the bureau.

To keep track of the dispute process:

1. **Document Everything:** Keep copies of your dispute letter, supporting documents, and any correspondence from the credit bureau or creditor.

2. **Follow-up:** If you are still waiting to hear back from the credit bureau within 45 days, follow up to check the status of your dispute.

## 3.4 Ensuring Errors are Corrected

If the creditor agrees the information is incorrect or cannot verify it, they must notify all three credit bureaus so they can correct the information in your credit report. The credit bureau should also provide a free copy of your updated credit report. Review it again to ensure that the errors have been fixed.

Ensuring your credit report is accurate is crucial to maintaining a healthy credit score. Diligence, patience, and organization are vital in identifying and rectifying errors on your credit report.

# Chapter 4: Debt Management, Creating a Successful Strategy

*"Debt management is a journey, not a sprint; it requires strategic planning, disciplined execution, and a commitment to change one's financial habits for a lifetime of credit health."*

## 4.1 Understanding the Impact of Debt on Your Credit Score

While taking on debt isn't necessarily a bad thing, how you manage that debt can significantly impact your credit score. High debt levels, especially credit card debt, can lower your score. Also, late or missed payments on any debt will negatively impact your credit history, which is a significant component of your credit score.

## 4.2 Prioritizing Different Types of Debt

Not all debts are created equal, and it's essential to understand which ones to prioritize:

- **Secured Debts:** These are loans secured by an asset, like a home or car. Defaulting on these loans can lead to the loss of the investment, so they should generally be prioritized.

- **High-Interest Debts:** Credit card debt usually carries a higher interest rate than other types of debt and allowing it to build up can be costly.

- **Student Loans:** While student loans typically have lower interest rates, they are rarely dischargeable in bankruptcy, making them a priority.

- **Medical Debts:** These don't carry interest and often involve no action unless you fail to pay, allowing you to focus on other, more pressing debts first.

## 4.3 Negotiating with Creditors

If you need help to keep up with payments, contact your creditors. Many may be willing to work out a payment plan, lower their interest rate, or even settle for a lower amount. Be honest about your situation, and remember, it's in your best interest to get paid, even if it's not the total amount.

## 4.4 The Role of Debt Consolidation

Debt consolidation involves taking out a new loan to pay off multiple debts. The goal is to secure a lower interest rate, a fixed interest rate, or to simplify your debt management. It's only for some, but it can be beneficial if you have high-interest credit card debt spread across multiple cards. However, debt consolidation requires discipline. You'll be worse if you accumulate more debt after consolidating. It's essential to have a budget and a plan for not getting more debt if you decide to take this route.

Debt management isn't about quick fixes. It's about creating a long-term strategy that fits your financial situation. You can manage your debt effectively and improve your credit score with careful planning and discipline. Remember, the goal isn't just to get out of debt; it's to stay out of debt.

# Chapter 5: Paying on Time, Building a History of Responsible Credit Usage

"Paying on time is more than a financial obligation; it's a testament to your financial responsibility, painting a picture of trustworthiness to lenders that can open doors to future opportunities."

## 5.1 The Importance of Timely Payments

The single most significant factor in determining your credit score is your payment history - it accounts for approximately 35% of your FICO score. Therefore, consistently making your credit payments on time is one of the most effective ways to improve your credit score and demonstrate responsible credit usage.

## 5.2 Setting Up Automatic Payments

Automatic payments can be a helpful tool in ensuring your payments are always made on time. Most lenders, banks, and credit card companies offer an option to deduct the minimum payment automatically, or more if you choose, from your bank account each month. This ensures you never miss a payment, even if it slips your mind. However, it's essential to make sure you always have sufficient funds in your account to cover these payments.

## 5.3 Using Budgeting Tools

Budgeting tools can also be instrumental in managing your payments. Many apps and digital platforms offer features that allow you to track your bills, send reminders when payments are due, and even budget your income and expenses. These tools ensure you always have funds available when it's time to pay your bills.

## 5.4 Managing Your Money Effectively

Effective money management is a crucial aspect of making timely payments. This involves understanding your income and expenses, creating, and sticking to a budget, and setting aside money for emergencies. By managing your money effectively, you always have the necessary funds to cover your debt payments, which helps build a solid credit history.

Paying your debts on time demonstrates to lenders that you're a low-risk borrower who will likely manage credit responsibly. Creating systems that make timely payments easier and managing your money effectively lays a solid foundation for a strong credit score. Remember, consistency is vital in credit - it's not just about making one payment on time, but all of them.

# Chapter 6: Credit Utilization 30% Rule

"Credit utilization is a balance game; maintaining under 30% is a quiet declaration of your creditworthiness to potential lenders."

## 6.1 Understanding Credit Utilization

The credit utilization ratio measures how much of your available credit you're using. It's calculated by dividing your total credit card balances by your total credit card limits. For example, if you have a total credit limit of $10,000 across all your cards and used $3,000, your credit utilization ratio is 30%.

## 6.2 The Importance of Credit Utilization

Credit utilization is a significant factor in your credit score, accounting for approximately 30% of your FICO score. Lenders see a low credit utilization ratio as an indicator that you're managing your credit well and not overextending yourself.

## 6.3 The 30% Rule

Keeping your credit utilization below 30% is recommended as a general guideline. This is known as the 30% rule. This doesn't mean you can't ever go above 30%, but consistently maintaining a lower ratio could positively impact your credit score.

## 6.4 Strategies to Control Credit Utilization

Here are several strategies to help keep your credit utilization low:

1. **Pay Your Balances in Full Each Month:** This is the best way to keep your credit utilization low. It means you're not carrying debt from month to month, and you're not paying interest.

2.  **Make Multiple Payments Throughout the Month:** If you use your credit card for most purchases, consider making multiple monthly payments to keep the balance low.

3.  **Increase Your Credit Limit:** If you can manage more credit responsibly, consider requesting a credit limit increase from your credit card issuer. This can lower your credit utilization ratio by increasing your available credit.

4.  **Don't Close Unused Credit Cards:** Unless a card has an annual fee that's not worth paying, it can be beneficial to keep the card open. The available credit on that card contributes to your overall credit limit, which can help keep your utilization rate low.

Keeping your credit utilization low is a long-term commitment and involves diligent monitoring of your credit balances. However, the effort can pay off through a healthier credit score and more significant future credit opportunities.

# Chapter 7: Diversifying Your Credit

*"Diversified credit reflects your financial wisdom; it's the art of balancing variety with responsible repayment over time."*

## 7.1 Understanding Different Types of Credit

Credit types are usually classified into two categories: revolving and installment.

1. **Revolving Credit:** This type of credit, including credit cards and lines of credit, has a limit, and you can borrow against it as many times as you like if you have available credit.

2. **Installment Credit:** This includes things like mortgages, auto loans, and student loans. You borrow a set amount of money and repay it with interest in equal installments over a specified term.

## 7.2 The Importance of Credit Mix

Credit mix — having various types of credit accounts for about 10% of your FICO score. Lenders like to see that you can manage different types of credit, so having a mix can improve your score.

## 7.3 Understanding Credit Age

Credit age refers to how long you've been using credit. It's determined by looking at the age of your oldest account and the average age of all your accounts. This forms part of your credit history and accounts for about 15% of your FICO score.

## 7.4 The Benefits of a Varied and Lengthy Credit History

A longer credit history can be beneficial because it provides more information about your spending habits and how you handle debt. It shows lenders that you can manage credit over the long term. A diverse credit portfolio indicates to lenders that you can responsibly manage different types of credit. If you only have one type of credit, consider diversifying. For instance, consider taking out a small personal or auto loan if you only have credit cards.

## 7.5 Building a Diverse Credit Portfolio Responsibly

While diversifying can be beneficial, it's crucial not to take out credit you don't need or can't afford to diversify. The most important thing is to manage your credit responsibly by paying on time and keeping balances low.

Credit variety and duration are critical elements of your credit profile. Understanding and managing these aspects can help ensure a robust and healthy credit score. Always remember responsible credit behavior over time is the key to a new credit record and a perfect 850 score.

# Chapter 8: The Art of Applying for New Credit

*"Applying for credit is a strategic move; done wisely, it propels you forward; done poorly, it can pull you back."*

## 8.1 Understanding Hard Inquiries

Hard inquiries occur when a lender or credit card issuer checks your credit as part of their lending decision. This typically happens when you apply for a loan, credit card, or mortgage. Each hard inquiry slightly lowers your credit score and stays on your credit report for two years.

## 8.2 Impact of Hard Inquiries on Your Credit Score

While a single hard inquiry may only slightly dent your credit score, multiple hard inquiries over a short period can add up and become a red flag for potential lenders. It can signal that you're desperately seeking credit or cannot secure the credit you need, both of which are risk indicators.

## 8.3 Strategies to Minimize Hard Inquiries

1. **Apply for New Credit Sparingly:** Only apply for new credit accounts when necessary. It's also important to space out your applications to avoid giving lenders the impression that you're desperate for credit.

2. **Pre-Qualify When Possible:** Many lenders and credit card issuers allow you to check if you pre-qualify for their products. These pre-qualifications usually involve a soft inquiry, which doesn't impact your credit score.

3. **Understand Your Creditworthiness:** Knowing your credit score and what type of credit products you're likely to qualify for can help you avoid applying for the credit you're unlikely to get.

## 8.4 When to Apply for New Credit

Your needs should drive the decision to apply for new credit rather than the desire to improve your credit mix or access more available credit. Before applying, consider the potential impact on your credit score and your ability to manage the additional credit.

## 8.5 Handling Rejections

If you're denied credit, you'll receive an "adverse action" letter from the lender explaining why. Use this information to understand what factors are affecting your creditworthiness and work on improving those areas.

Remember, hard inquiries are just one aspect of your credit profile. While essential, they carry less weight than high credit card balances or late payments. The key to a perfect credit score is a long history of on-time payments, low balances, and prudent credit management.

# Chapter 9: Recovering from Major Credit Issues, Bankruptcy and Foreclosure

*"Major credit issues are not the end; with patience and discipline, you can rewrite your financial story towards success."*

## 9.1 The Impact of Major Credit Problems

Significant credit issues like bankruptcy, foreclosure, and repossession can severely impact your credit score, and the adverse effects can linger for years. However, it's essential to remember that these impacts are not permanent and that recovery is possible.

## 9.2 Bankruptcy and Your Credit

Bankruptcy is a legal process to relieve individuals or businesses struggling with unmanageable debt. However, it has the most severe impact on your credit score and remains on your credit report for seven to ten years, depending on the type of bankruptcy filed.

## 9.3 Foreclosure and Repossession

Foreclosure occurs when a lender takes possession of a property due to the homeowner's failure to make mortgage payments. Repossession is when a lender takes back an item bought on credit, like a car, due to non-payment. These events can dramatically lower your credit score and stay on your credit report for seven years.

## 9.4 Strategies for Rebuilding Credit

Rebuilding credit after major problems requires time, patience, and responsible financial behavior. Here are some strategies to help you rebuild:

1. **Pay All Bills on Time:** Consistently paying bills on time will rebuild your credit history with positive information.

2. **Establish a Budget:** Keep spending under control and prioritize saving to avoid future financial hardships.

3. **Use Credit Wisely:** To build a positive credit history, apply for a secured credit card or small installment loan. Always pay on time and keep balances low.

4. **Monitor Your Credit:** Regularly check your credit report to ensure its accurate and that your positive behaviors are correctly reported.

## 9.5 Mitigating the Impact of Major Credit Problems

You can mitigate the impact of significant credit problems on your credit score by staying current with other debts, communicating with your lenders, and exploring alternatives such as loan modifications or selling your property.

Though major credit issues can be a significant setback, they don't define your financial future. With patience, perseverance, and a commitment to responsible financial habits, you can gradually restore your credit health and progress towards that coveted 850 score.

# Chapter 10: Best Practices and Habits to Maintain a High Credit Score

*"A high credit score isn't a destination but an ongoing journey of diligence, discipline, and responsible financial habits."*

## 10.1 Consistency is Key

Once you've reached your credit score goals, maintaining those numbers is paramount. This isn't achieved through one-off actions but by forming and sticking to responsible financial habits. Always remember that consistency is key.

## 10.2 Best Practices for High Credit Scores

**Pay on Time:** The most influential factor on your credit score is your payment history. Ensure all bills are paid on time, every time.

**Keep Balances Low:** Maintaining a low credit utilization ratio shows you responsibly manage your available credit.

**Maintain a Healthy Credit Mix:** A blend of installment and revolving credit can positively affect your credit score.

**Limit New Credit Applications:** Hard inquiries can impact your score. Limit new credit applications and only apply when necessary.

## 10.3 Avoiding Actions that Hurt Your Credit Score

Avoid late or missed payments, maxing out your credit cards, and applying for credit too frequently. All these actions can negatively impact your score. Remember, rebuilding your credit can take time, so avoiding any pitfalls that could set you back is essential.

## 10.4 The Ongoing Journey of Credit Management

Maintaining a high credit score is an ongoing journey, not a destination. It requires persistent attention to your financial habits, regular monitoring of your credit report, and a commitment to financial discipline.

Financial health is more than just a high credit score; it's about the freedom and opportunities that come with it. As you navigate the journey of credit management, remember to focus on building savings, investing for the future, and continuously educating yourself about personal finance.

You've acquired the knowledge and skills to achieve and maintain a perfect 850 credit score. Now, it's all about putting those skills into practice and making them a part of your financial routine. With consistency, patience, and diligence, you'll maintain that perfect score and build a stable and secure financial future.

# Chapter 11: Leveraging Online Tools to Remove Inaccuracies and Hard Inquiries

## 11.1 Understanding Hard Inquiries

Hard inquiries occur when a lender or credit card issuer checks your credit as part of their decision-making process. These inquiries can slightly lower your credit score and remain on your credit report for two years. While one or two hard inquiries aren't likely to significantly affect your credit score, multiple ones can.

## 11.2 Disputing Hard Inquiries

Sometimes, a hard inquiry might occur without your approval, or a mistake happens, and an inquiry might appear multiple times. In such cases, you have the right to dispute the hard inquiry. This process can be done manually or through online tools.

## 11.3 Manual Dispute Letters

The traditional way to dispute hard inquiries is by writing a letter to the credit bureau that reported the inquiry. This letter should include your name, address, the hard inquiry you're disputing, and the reason for the dispute.

**11.4 Online Dispute Tools**

Many online tools are available to facilitate the dispute process, which can be faster and more efficient. Here are some worth exploring:

**1. Credit Bureau Online Portals:** Equifax, Experian, and TransUnion all offer online portals where you can dispute inaccuracies on your credit report, including hard inquiries.

• **Transunion:** https://www.transunion.com/credit-disputes/dispute-your-credit#

• **Experian:** https://www.experian.com/disputes/main.html

• **Equifax:** https://www.equifax.com/personal/credit-report-services/credit-dispute/

**2. Credit Monitoring Services:** Many credit monitoring services, like Credit Karma and Credit Sesame, offer tools for disputing errors on your credit report. These services can also help you keep track of changes to your credit score and report.

• **Credit Karma:** www.creditkarma.com

• **Credit Sesame:** www.creditsesame.com

**3. Automated Dispute Platforms:** Some online platforms automate the dispute process. You input some information, and the platform generates a dispute letter and sends it to the appropriate credit bureau.

• **Credit Versio:** https://www.creditversio.com/
Many companies offering credit repair services leverage Credit Versio's platform and significantly mark the cost up. Instead of investing hundreds or even thousands of

dollars in costly programs that claim to fix your credit, you can take control of your financial health independently for a mere starting price of $19.99. This affordable, self-guided approach is a secret that many credit gurus hesitate to reveal.

**Note:** We will cover this more in detail in upcoming chapters.

## 11.5 Credit Repair Software

You may want to consider credit repair software if dealing with multiple credit issues, including hard inquiries. These platforms can identify negative items on your credit report, guide you through the dispute process, and provide tips and resources for improving your credit.

Remember, each hard inquiry listed on your credit report must be authorized by you. If you find hard inquiries, you did not authorize, or if they're duplicated, don't hesitate to dispute them. Be proactive in managing your credit, and leverage the online tools and resources available to maintain your financial health.

## Figure 1: Example of Dispute letter to remove inquires

[Your Name]

[Your Address]

[City, State, Zip]

[Email Address]

[Phone Number]

[Date]


[Credit Bureau Name]

[Credit Bureau Address]

[City, State, Zip]


Subject: Request for Removal of Unauthorized Inquiries


Dear Sir/Madam,


I recently reviewed my credit report and found several hard inquiries I did not authorize. Unauthorized hard inquiries are a serious matter, and they can impact my credit score.

Here are the unauthorized inquiries that I found:

[Name of Lender or Company making the inquiry], [Date of Inquiry]

[Name of Lender or Company making the inquiry], [Date of Inquiry]

[Name of Lender or Company making the inquiry], [Date of Inquiry]

(Add as many as necessary)

As per the Fair Credit Reporting Act, I did not provide any of these companies with the permissible purpose of inquiring into my credit report. Therefore, I request that these hard inquiries be removed from my credit report immediately.

Please find the relevant pages from my credit report highlighting the inquiries in question. I trust that your agency will handle this request promptly to ensure the accuracy of my credit report.

I would appreciate a written confirmation from you once the removal of these unauthorized inquiries has been completed. If any further actions are required from me, please inform me.

Thank you for your attention to this matter.

Sincerely,

[Your Name]

Enclosures: (Mention any documents you are sending with the letter, such as copies of the credit report, etc.)

In the next chapter, we will introduce a program that will do all this work for you.

# Chapter 12: Leveraging Credit Versio to Repair Your Credit Report

Credit Versio is a renowned platform designed to aid individuals in improving their credit scores. It employs sophisticated algorithms and artificial intelligence to identify errors in credit reports and suggests actionable steps for rectification. In this chapter, we'll guide you through the process of utilizing Credit Versio to mend your credit effectively.

**Step 1: Creating an Account**

- **Navigate to the Website:** Visit the official Credit Versio website at https://www.creditversio.com/

- **Sign Up:** Click on the "Sign Up" button and fill in the necessary details including your name, email address, and password.

- **Verify Email:** Check your inbox for a verification email and confirm your account.

**Step 2: Uploading Credit Reports**

- **Obtain Credit Reports:** Secure copies of your credit reports from the three major credit bureaus: Equifax, Experian, and TransUnion. Credit Versio is partnered with Credit Smart so they will also allow you to purchase your reports within the site.

- **Upload Documents:** Log in to your Credit Versio account and upload the obtained credit reports.

## Step 3: Analyzing Credit Reports

- **Automated Analysis:** Once uploaded, Credit Versio's AI will automatically analyze your reports to detect discrepancies, inaccuracies, and areas of improvement.
- **Review Findings:** Carefully review the detailed findings and suggestions provided by the platform.

## Step 4: Disputing Errors

- **Select Discrepancies:** Identify and select the inaccuracies you wish to dispute.
- **Generate Dispute Letters:** Credit Versio will generate customized dispute letters for each selected item.

- **Send Dispute Letters:** Mail the generated dispute letters to the respective credit bureaus, and keep copies for your records.

## Step 5: Monitoring Progress

- **Track Disputes:** Use your Credit Versio dashboard to monitor the status of your disputes and any responses from the credit bureaus.
- **Update Information:** Update any necessary information on your account, based on the progress of your disputes.

## Step 6: Reviewing Updated Credit Reports

- **Receive Updated Reports:** Once the disputes are resolved, obtain updated credit reports from the credit bureaus.
- **Verify Corrections:** Verify that the inaccuracies have been corrected and that your credit score has been adjusted accordingly.

## Step 7: Implementing Recommendations

- **Follow Credit Improvement Recommendations:** Implement the personalized credit improvement recommendations provided by Credit Versio.
- **Consistently Review Credit:** Regularly review your credit reports to ensure that all information remains accurate and to catch any future discrepancies early.

Leveraging Credit Versio can significantly streamline the process of repairing your credit. By following the steps and consistently monitoring your credit reports, you can ensure the accuracy of your financial records and work towards improving your credit score. Please note that the platform's effectiveness depends on accurate and up-to-date user inputs and responsible financial habits. Regularly using Credit Versio and adhering to its recommendations will foster financial responsibility and creditworthiness in the long run.

# Chapter 13: Enhancing Your Credit as an Authorized User

The world of credit can often seem intricate, with numerous avenues to explore. One effective yet lesser-known strategy is becoming an authorized user on someone else's credit card. But what does that entail, and how can it potentially boost your credit? This chapter delves into the advantages, caveats, and the process of becoming an authorized user.

## 13.1 Understanding the Role of an Authorized User

**Definition**: An authorized user is a person who is granted permission to use another individual's credit card. This user is authorized to make purchases but isn't responsible for the accumulated debt.

## 13.2 Potential Credit Benefits

- **Credit History Boost**: If the primary cardholder has a positive credit history, this can reflect favorably on the authorized user's credit report.

- **Increased Credit Age**: The length of credit history accounts for 15% of a FICO score. Being added to an older account can instantly age your credit.

- **Improved Credit Utilization**: The authorized user could benefit from a lower credit utilization rate if the primary cardholder maintains a low balance.

## 13.3 Process of Being Added as an Authorized User

- **Select the Right Primary Cardholder**: This should ideally be someone with a long, positive credit history and responsible financial habits.

- **Approach the Cardholder**: Discuss the implications, and your reasons for the request, and assure them of your intention to use the card responsibly (if you're granted access).

- **Formal Request**: The primary cardholder will need to contact their credit card issuer and provide your details to add you.

- **Wait for the Credit Card**: Once added, you'll either receive a card with your name or share one with the primary cardholder.

## 13.4 Pros of Becoming an Authorized User

- **Credit Score Boost**: As mentioned, a well-managed account can uplift your score.

- **No Liability**: You aren't legally bound to pay off the card's debt.

- **Learning Opportunity**: For those new to credit, this offers a chance to understand credit dynamics without major risks.

## 13.5 Cons of Becoming an Authorized User

- **Primary Holder's Financial Habits Impact You**: If they max out the card or miss payments, it can negatively affect your credit.

- **Reduced Autonomy**: Spending decisions might need approval from the primary cardholder.

- **Potential Strain on Relationships**: Money matters can strain personal relationships if not handled carefully.

## 13.6 When to Consider Removal as an Authorized User

- **Negative Reporting**: If the account reflects negatively on your credit report due to the primary cardholder's actions.

- **Achieving Independence**: Once you've built a decent credit history and can get your own credit card.

*To be removed, contact the credit card issuer with your request. Ensure the account is removed from your credit report by checking it post-removal.

## 13.7 Important Considerations

- **Not All Issuers Report Authorized User Activity**: Ensure the issuer reports authorized user activity to the credit bureaus before being added.

- **Communication is Key**: Discuss any spending, limits, and expectations upfront.

- **Monitor Your Credit**: Regularly check to ensure the account is benefiting your credit history.

Becoming an authorized user can be a beneficial stepping stone in the credit journey, especially for those starting or looking to rebuild. However, it's crucial to approach it with a full understanding and open communication. The primary cardholder and the authorized user must be on the same page to ensure this arrangement is fruitful and free from misunderstandings. Remember, the world of credit offers many paths; being an authorized user is just one of many routes to a robust credit score.

# Chapter 14: Rebuilding your Credit with Self Inc.

## 14.1 Introduction:

In the modern financial landscape, establishing and building credit is of paramount importance. Enter Self Inc., a financial technology company designed to aid individuals in this endeavor. This chapter sheds light on the advantages of utilizing Self Inc. and provides a roadmap to leveraging its services for credit-building.

## 14.2 An Overview of Self Inc

Self-Inc., often simply referred to as "Self," operates with a mission to help consumers establish and improve their credit scores. Through its unique credit-builder loans and secured credit card offerings, Self offers a structured pathway to credit enhancement, especially for those who might struggle with traditional banking systems.

## 14.3 The Mechanics of Self's Credit Builder Loan

**Secured Loans**: Instead of giving you the loan amount upfront, Self keeps the loan in a Certificate of Deposit (CD) which is FDIC-insured.

- **Scheduled Payments**: You make monthly payments towards the loan. These payments include both the loan amount and interest charges.

- **Credit Reporting**: As you make payments, Self reports your activity to all three major credit bureaus.

- **Access to Funds**: Once the loan term is completed, the CD unlocks, and the money (minus the interest and fees) is yours.

## 14.4 Advantages of Using Self

- **No Hard Credit Check**: Applying for the credit builder loan doesn't result in a hard inquiry, ensuring your existing score isn't impacted.

- **Flexible Loan Amounts and Terms**: Choose from various loan amounts and repayment terms to find a fit for your budget.

- **Reports to All Major Bureaus**: Regular reporting means your on-time payments help in building your credit history.

- **Secured Credit Card**: After making a few payments, you can qualify for Self's secured credit card, offering another avenue to build credit.

- **Online Accessibility**: Manage your loan, track progress, and access resources through Self's intuitive platform.

## 14.5 Steps to Build Credit with Self

- **Sign Up**: Visit Self's official website to create an account here: **https://self.inc/refer/TGN1YFUF**

- **Choose a Loan Plan**: Based on your financial comfort, pick a loan amount and term.

- **Make Regular Payments**: Ensure you pay the monthly amount on time.

- **Monitor Your Credit**: Use the platform to track your credit score changes over time.

- **Graduate to Self's Secured Card**: After demonstrating consistent payments, consider applying for Self's secured credit card to further enhance your credit-building efforts.

- **Complete Your Loan Term**: At the end of the term, access the funds from the CD.

## 14.6: Things to Remember

- **Consistency is Key**: Like all credit-building methods, consistency in payments is vital.
- **Be Aware of Fees**: Understand any associated fees, like the administrative fee Self charges at the beginning.
- **Secured Card Deposit**: If you opt for the secured card, remember that a portion of your CD will act as the card's security deposit.
- **Stay Informed**: Make use of Self Inc. educational resources to stay informed about credit-building best practices.

Building credit can seem daunting, especially for those new to it or recovering from financial setbacks. Self Inc. offers a structured, user-friendly, and transparent approach to this challenge. By understanding its workings and making diligent and informed choices, individuals can harness Self Inc. as a potent tool in their credit-building journey.

# 90-Day Checklist for Building Your Credit Score

## Days 1-10: Setting the Groundwork

[ ] **Obtain Credit Reports**: Secure copies from all three major credit bureaus: Equifax, Experian, and TransUnion.

[ ] **Review for Inaccuracies**: Thoroughly check your reports for any discrepancies or errors.

[ ] **Dispute Errors**: Report any inaccuracies to the respective credit bureaus.

[ ] **Set Up Payment Reminders**: Ensure you never miss a due date by setting up reminders or enabling auto-pay where feasible.

**Log**: Note starting credit score, any discrepancies found, and debts reviewed.

**Days 11-30: Addressing Credit Utilization and Reducing Debt**

[ ] **Understand Your Credit Utilization Ratio**: It's the ratio of your credit card balances to their credit limits.

[ ] **Aim for 30% or Less**: Try to keep your utilization below this threshold.

[ ] **Reduce Debt**: Start by paying off outstanding balances on credit cards or loans.

[ ] **Avoid Multiple Card Applications**: Each hard inquiry can reduce your score.

**Log**: Track credit card balances and any changes to credit limits.

**Days 31-60: Diversifying Credit and Building Consistency**

[ ] **Understand Credit Mix**: Different types of credit (credit cards, mortgages, student loans) can positively impact your score.

[ ] **Consider a Secured Credit Card**: Only if you don't qualify for regular ones and ensure it reports to all three bureaus.

[ ] **Continue On-Time Payments**: This is the most significant factor in your credit score.

[ ] **Don't Close Old Accounts**: Age of credit impacts your score; older accounts can benefit you.

**Log**: Note any new credit accounts opened and document monthly debt reductions.

**Days 61-90: Exploring Advanced Strategies and Review**

[ ] **Consider Becoming an Authorized User**: Being added to a responsible payer's credit card account can boost your score.

[ ] **Explore Credit Boosting Programs**: Services like Experian Boost can consider utility bill payments in your credit score.

[ ] **Obtain Current Credit Reports**: Check the progress made over the past two months.

[ ] **Set Short-Term Financial Goals**: This can guide your credit use for the next few months.

**Log**: Document any score changes, note if you became an authorized user, or joined any boosting programs.

**End of 90-Day Period: Reflection**

Reflect on the progress made over the last three months. Understand areas of improvement, celebrate the strides taken, and chart the path forward. Achieving a high credit score in 90 days is ambitious; the key is establishing good habits that lead to long-term financial health.

# Credit Building Journal

## Personal Details Page:

Name: _____

Starting Date: _____

Goal Credit Score: _____

Current Credit Score: _____

6-Month Target Score: _____

12-Month Target Score: _____

## Monthly Log Pages:

**Month 1 (Date)** _____

**Credit Score at the Start of the Month:** _____

**Financial Goals for the Month:**

- _____

- _____

- _____

- _____

●  _____

**Activities & Actions:**

**Week 1**

**Payments Made:** (List all payments made, including amounts

and due dates).

_____

_____

_____

_____

**Discrepancies/Errors Found:** (If any were found on your

credit report).

_____

_____

_____

_____

_____

**Steps Taken to Rectify Errors:**

_____

_____

_____

_____

_____

**Week 2**

**Payments Made:**

_____

_____

_____

_____

_____

**New Inquiries/Credit Checks:**

---

---

---

---

---

**Week 3**

**Payments Made:**

---

---

---

---

---

**Credit Utilization:** (List your current balances versus your

credit limits)

_____

_____

_____

_____

_____

## Week 4

**Payments Made:**

_____

_____

_____

_____

_____

**Any New Lines of Credit Opened:** (If applicable)

_____

_____

_____

_____

**End-of-Month Review:** _____

**Credit Score at End of Month:** _____

**Achievements:** (Any positive changes or behaviors you

noticed)

_____

_____

_____

_____

**Areas for Improvement:** (Any missed payments, high

utilization rates, etc.)

_____

_____

_____

_____

**Goals for Next Month:**

- _____

- _____

- _____

- _____

- _____

# Month 2 (Date) _____

## Credit Score at the Start of the Month: _____

## Financial Goals for the Month:

- _____

- _____

- _____

- _____

- _____

## Activities & Actions:

## Week 1

**Payments Made:** (List all payments made, including amounts

and due dates).

_____

_____

_____

_____

_____

**Discrepancies/Errors Found:** (If any were found on your

credit report).

_____

_____

_____

_____

_____

**Steps Taken to Rectify Errors:**

_____

_____

_____

_____

_____

## Week 2

**Payments Made:**

_____

_____

_____

_____

_____

**New Inquiries/Credit Checks:**

_____

_____

_____

_____

_____

## Week 3

**Payments Made:**

_____

_____

_____

_____

_____

**Credit Utilization:** (List your current balances versus your

credit limits)

_____

_____

_____

_____

_____

## Week 4

**Payments Made:**

_____

_____

_____

_____

_____

**Any New Lines of Credit Opened:** (If applicable)

_____

_____

_____

_____

_____

**End-of-Month Review:** _____

**Credit Score at End of Month:** _____

**Achievements:** (Any positive changes or behaviors you

noticed)

_____

_____

_____

_____

_____

**Areas for Improvement:** (Any missed payments, high

utilization rates, etc.)

_____

_____

_____

_____

_____

# Goals for Next Month:

- _____

- _____

- _____

- _____

- _____

# Month 3 (Date) _____

**Credit Score at the Start of the Month:** _____

**Financial Goals for the Month:**

- _____

- _____

- _____

- _____

- _____

**Activities & Actions:**

## Week 1

**Payments Made:** (List all payments made, including amounts

and due dates).

_____

_____

_____

_____

_____

**Discrepancies/Errors Found:** (If any were found on your

credit report).

_____

_____

_____

_____

**Steps Taken to Rectify Errors:**

_____

_____

_____

_____

## Week 2

**Payments Made:**

_____

_____

_____

_____

**New Inquiries/Credit Checks:**

_____

_____

_____

_____

## Week 3

**Payments Made:**

_____

_____

_____

_____

_____

**Credit Utilization:** (List your current balances versus your credit limits)

_____

_____

_____

_____

## Week 4

**Payments Made:**

_____

_____

_____

_____

_____

**Any New Lines of Credit Opened:** (If applicable)

_____

_____

_____

_____

_____

**End-of-Month Review:** _____

**Credit Score at End of Month:** _____

**Achievements:** (Any positive changes or behaviors you

noticed)

_____

_____

_____

_____

**Areas for Improvement:** (Any missed payments, high

utilization rates, etc.)

_____

_____

_____

_____

**Goals for Next Month:**

- _____

- _____

- _____

- _____

- _____


Repeat the monthly log format for each month or as long as you need to track your progress.

# Yearly Reflection Page

**Credit Score at the Start of the Year:** _____

**Credit Score at End of Year:** _____

**Major Milestones Achieved:** (Paid off a credit card, reduced

total debt by a certain percentage, etc.)

1. _____

2. _____

3. _____

4. _____

5. _____


**Challenges Faced:**

1. _____

2. _____

3. _____

4. _____

5. _____

**Goals for Next Year:**

1. _____

2. _____

3. _____

4. _____

5. _____

**Resources & Contacts Page:**

**Credit Bureaus' Contact Information:**

**Equifax:**

Phone:

Address:

**Experian:**

Phone:

Address:

**TransUnion:**

Phone:

Address:

**Other Important Contacts:** (e.g., financial advisor, bank, etc.)

Financial Advisor:


Bank:



Using this journal consistently can give you an organized view of your credit-building journey. Review it frequently, update it diligently, and always aim to set clear, achievable goals.